20 Answers

❧

Atheism

Matt Fradd

Catholic
Answers
Press

20 Answers Atheism

Matt Fradd

© 2014 Catholic Answers

Published by Catholic Answers, Inc.

2020 Gillespie Way

El Cajon, California 92020

1-888-291-8000 orders

619-387-0042 fax

catholic.com

Printed in the United States of America

ISBN 978-1-938983-52-8 paperback

ISBN 978-1-938983-53-5 Kindle

ISBN 978-1-938983-54-2 ePub

TOTUS TUUS MARIA

A short and simple book deserves a short and simple blurb. I am happy to supply it for Matt Fradd's useful little book, *20 Answers: Atheism*. It is practical, to the point, and on target. Above all, it's TRUE.
—*Peter Kreeft, Professor of Philosophy, Boston College*

Introduction

A few years ago, in England, there were brightly colored ads on the sides of buses, sponsored by atheist groups, that read, "There's probably no God. Now stop worrying and enjoy your life."

Well, we could try. But it might not be that easy. For no question is more important than "Does God exist?"

If God does not exist, then we must admit—however unpleasant the thought may be—that there is ultimately nothing special about the world and the beings that inhabit it. Mankind is merely the product of a random and senseless cosmic process: the result of time plus matter plus chance. As one atheist put it, we're all just "bags of chemical reactions walking around." We can pretend that there is meaning to life, but this amounts to nothing more than self-delusion. In the end, nothing matters.

As the famous atheist author Bertrand Russell remarked:

All the labors of the ages, all the devotion, all the inspiration, all the noonday brightness of human genius, are destined to extinction in the vast death of the solar system, and that the whole temple of Man's achievement must inevitably be buried beneath the debris of a universe in ruins—all these things, if not quite beyond dispute, are yet so nearly certain, that no philosophy which rejects them can hope to stand.[1]

That bus ad is just one example of a recent surge of anti-evangelism by a new and aggressive form of unbelief. The zeal of the so-called "new atheists"—such as Richard Dawkins and the late Christopher Hitchens—is enough to put even the most enthusiastic televangelist to shame.

I have a lot of sympathy for people who don't believe in God. I used to be in that position myself, and for a long time no one gave me good answers to the questions and concerns I had. But I have since discovered that there *are* good answers—that there are good arguments for God's existence.

In the pages that follow, we will look at twenty common questions and objections that atheists pose— that *I* used to pose—and offer solid theistic answers. Whether you are an atheist, an agnostic, or a believer, it's my sincere hope that this booklet will help you as you study the issue of God's existence.

After all, there is no bigger question.

1. Atheism is not a positive proposition, so it does not have to be proven. The burden of proof is always on the theist.

Theism, which is derived from the Greek word for God, *theos*, is the view that God exists. Atheism, in contrast, is the view that God does not exist. That means atheism is a claim to knowledge—not merely a suspension of belief. In other words, an atheist is a person who *rejects* the existence of God, not a person who isn't sure if God exists or who is waiting to see more proof. We already have a perfectly good word in the English language for a person who withholds belief in God: agnostic.

Some atheists want to redefine atheism as something more like agnosticism, so they won't have to prove their position. This eagerness to redefine atheism all but admits the weakness of arguments against God's existence. If atheists thought these arguments were compelling, they would spend less time on redefining words instead.

The person who is trying to convince someone else of his position must always shoulder the burden of proof. If I want to convince someone to abandon the belief that there is no good evidence for God and come to believe that theism is true, then I bear the burden of proof. But this applies to atheists as well. If they want to convince me to abandon my belief that there *is* good evidence for God and come to believe that *atheism* is true, then they must offer proof. The rejection of God is as much a claim to knowledge as belief in God.

2. I can't prove atheism because it is impossible to "prove a negative." To do that, I would have to know

every single thing in reality and demonstrate that none of these things is God. That's humanly impossible.

It's entirely possible to "prove a negative." People do it all the time.

For example, you can prove that there are no square circles, or that there are no lions in the room with you right now, or that there are no flaming snowflakes (as awesome or terrifying as that might be).

In fact, the claim "There are no negative propositions that can be proved" is itself a negative proposition! So any argument in favor of it can't work, because that would undermine the claim it's attempting to prove.

You don't have to scan everything in the universe to determine that there is no God to be found. If the idea of God is nonsensical, as atheists often claim, then you could demonstrate it logically the same way that you can demonstrate that there are no square circles. A mathematician doesn't have to search every inch of the universe to make sure there aren't any square circles hiding in it. Geometry tells him there aren't.

On the other hand, if the idea of God *isn't* nonsensical, then the atheist must provide evidence to show why a believer should conclude that God doesn't exist. He must also refute the arguments that seek to prove God does exist. The traditional arguments for God's existence don't amount to "You can't prove there is not a God; therefore there must be a God!" Rather, they offer positive reasons for believing in God as the universe's creator, designer, moral lawgiver, first cause, and so forth.

3. Christians sometimes argue that God is the basis of morality. But can't an atheist be just as good a person as a believer?

A person can certainly follow personal or social codes of morality even if he doesn't believe in God. However, without God there would be no foundation for *objective* morality—that is a reason to explain why some actions just *are* right or wrong regardless of what some people may think or do.

Many atheists actually agree on this point. The French atheist philosopher Jean-Paul Sartre said that it's "extremely embarrassing that God does not exist, for there disappears all possibility of finding values in an intelligible heaven."[2] But other atheists disagree with this, usually in one of two ways. First, they may claim that there are no objective truths and that morality is simply relative. They don't believe that even great evils like the Holocaust are objectively wrong—just that they are wrong from their own point of view. But if you believe that the Holocaust or other evils such as torture or rape just are wrong, no matter what anyone thinks, then this solution won't work for you. The second option for an atheist is to argue that objective morality does exist but is not grounded in God (we'll examine that argument in a little bit).

Other atheists vacillate, acknowledging that their worldview makes no room for objective morality but then turning around and speaking as if right and wrong were real. For example, celebrity atheist Richard Dawkins writes, "The universe that we observe has precisely the properties we should expect if there is, at bottom, no design, no purpose, no evil, no good, nothing but pitiless indifference."[3] But then elsewhere he writes that "faith is one of the world's great evils, comparable to the smallpox virus but harder to eradicate."[4] So which is it? Does evil exist or not?

So atheists can be morally good people. In fact, some atheists are more moral than some people who believe in God. But there still needs to be an objective ground for morality. The atheist worldview does not provide one, but the Christian one does: It is God himself.

4. How can God exist when religion is the number-one source of hatred, intolerance, and violence in the world?

Although I don't concede for a moment that "religion is the number-one source" of those things, it needs to be understood that a belief's effects on society don't tell us whether that belief is true.

For example, the Soviet dictator Joseph Stalin ruled over an atheistic regime that killed tens of millions of people. That was an enormous crime against humanity, but we can't conclude from it that atheism is false and so there must be a God. Likewise we can't take crimes committed in God's name as proof that he doesn't exist.

5. Religious believers don't care about people on earth because they are so focused on heaven.

This objection loses its force when we realize that many religious people view the afterlife as being intimately connected to their earthly life. As a result, their belief in heaven (and hell) is also a powerful motivator to do good in *this* world. The Bible, for example, stresses that part of religious faith is doing good works on earth. (See, for example, the parable of the sheep and the goats in Matthew 25:31-46, where Jesus sends the sheep who loved their neighbor to eternal happiness and the goats who did not to eternal damnation.)

Accordingly, throughout history religions have done enormous earthly good: feeding the hungry, caring for the sick, assisting the poor, and fighting injustice. It was churches and religious believers who founded the first schools, hospitals, charities, and other institutions focused on improving life on earth. The belief that God has commanded you to help other people because they are made in God's image and have intrinsic value, and the corresponding belief that it is wrong to disobey an infinite and morally perfect being like God, are powerful incentives to do good even at a high personal cost to oneself!

On the other hand, atheism can be a powerful *dis*-incentive to doing good things for others, especially those that come at a high personal cost. If an atheist were consistent in his principles, then he would acknowledge, as scientist Victor Stenger did, that "the earth is no more significant than a single grain of sand on a vast beach."[5]

If atheism were true, then I would agree with Stenger: The earth, and consequently mankind, is ultimately insignificant, and life is meaningless. In that case, why spend time and energy doing good for anyone but yourself? As Peter Kreeft and Ronald Tacelli write,

Concern for heavenly things does not devalue or demean concern for earthly things for the same reason a pregnant woman's concern for her baby's future does not devalue, detract, or distract from her concern for her baby's present. If she believed that her baby was going to be born dead (i.e., wanted an abortion), then the baby's life would be demeaned and devalued, and she would cease to care for it. If we believe that life ends with death, like a cosmic abortion, then we will care for it not more but less than if we believe that it is a pregnancy that will bear eternity.[6]

Of course, the question of whether believers or atheists are more helpful to society doesn't tell us which viewpoint is true.

6. Isn't it arrogant for you to think that your views are the correct ones and that everyone else is wrong?

We should first remember that *all people* think their views are correct. If they didn't, they wouldn't hold those views. Even the person who believes that it is arrogant for people to "think that their views are the correct ones and that everyone else is wrong" thinks *he* is correct in saying so, and those who disagree with him on it are wrong. There is nothing arrogant about having good reasons for a belief and thus really believing what you believe. Just as much as theists believe they are correct when they say God exists and those who disagree are mistaken, atheists believe they are correct when they say God doesn't exist and that the theists are wrong.

It must be recognized, too, that most theists don't believe "everyone else is wrong." Although as a Christian, I don't agree with other religions when they conflict with Christianity, I can agree that there are elements of truth, often many important ones, in them. For example, I agree with Islam that one God exists, though I disagree with Muslims with their view of God's nature and how he has revealed himself.

An atheist, on the other hand, must believe that the major claims of *all* religions are utterly false and that those who believe those claims are deluded. He must hold that only atheists are right about God and that the overwhelming majority of people who have ever lived have been completely wrong about what matters most to them.

Which sounds more tolerant to you?

7. How can we believe in God without scientific proof?

Science is a method for discovering truths about the natural world. But it has nothing to say about things *outside* the natural world—things that can't be observed or tested. Examining the material world, for example, can't disprove spiritual truths, such as the existence of an immaterial God. Even if science were to describe the physical universe exhaustively, it would still leave the question: Why does the universe, and the laws that govern it, exist?

Evolutionary biologist and atheist Steven Jay Gould sums it up nicely: "To say it for all my colleagues and for the umpteenth million time ... science simply cannot (by its legitimate methods) adjudicate the issue of God's possible superintendence of nature. We neither affirm nor deny it; we simply can't comment on it as scientists."[7]

True science recognizes the limits of its sphere of knowledge. The view that science can or should provide the answer to *every* question is not true science, but a corruption of science called scientism. It claims that we shouldn't accept as true anything that we can't prove scientifically.

Yet clearly there are many things science can't prove:

1. It can't prove the laws of logic, or mathematical truths—it merely presupposes them.
2. It can't prove metaphysical truths, such as the reality of the external world or that the universe did not simply spring into existence five minutes ago with the appearance of age, including our memories of a past that never happened. These are rational beliefs, but they can't be proven scientifically.
3. It can't prove morality. Science can't show that we have a duty to help a starving child or that Nazi concentration camps were evil. Good and evil are not material entities that can be measured in a laboratory; therefore their existence and nature are beyond what science can prove.

There is also this fact: If scientism were true, then it should be scientifically provable.

Is it?

No, because the claim "You shouldn't believe anything unless it is proven by science" is a philosophical
claim that you can't verify by any scientific experiment! Rather, it expresses a value judgment—what we
should choose to believe—placing it in the realm of
ethics and morals. We have already seen that science
can't verify the existence of immaterial moral truths.
This means that scientism is not only false, it is also
self-refuting, because it can't meet its own test.

8. What about evolution? Isn't that a scientific theory that contradicts the existence of God?

The theory of evolution proposes an explanation for how
life on earth arose and developed. It holds that there was
a long period in which natural processes gave rise to life
and that life changes over time from one generation to the
next. As life changes and adapts to survive in changing
environments, new creatures begin to emerge. According
to the theory of evolution, this process has given rise to all
the different life forms on earth, including man.

Whether true or false, this in no way conflicts with
the idea of God. As the omnipotent creator, God is
free to create quickly or slowly, directly or through
intermediate processes. He can create the universe in
an instantaneous Big Bang and then put it through a
long, slow period of development, giving rise to stars
and planets and eventually life forms. Since he directs

and sustains those processes, he can even intervene in them: such as when he creates a soul for each human being or when he performs a miracle.

Evolution is one way of explaining how life developed. But, like science itself, it is unable to answer the question: Why is there a universe with natural laws that allow evolutionary processes in the first place?

Consider an analogy: Suppose that after a thorough scientific investigation of the famous painting *Mona Lisa*, I concluded that it was the result of collisions of paint and canvas gradually leading from indecipherable shapes and patches of color to a beautiful and intriguing picture of a woman.

My analysis of the painting would be correct. That is, in fact, what the *Mona Lisa* is and how it developed. But my analysis by no means disproves or makes unnecessary Leonardo Da Vinci as the painter. And which seems more reasonable: that the collisions of paint and canvas occurred randomly until a masterpiece emerged, or that they were directed by some intelligence?

Consider one more thing. If *we* were the product of random evolutionary processes, without anyone directing them, then we'd have good reason to doubt our mental faculties when it comes to knowing the truth. Why? Because biologists tell us that evolutionary development is not aimed at producing true beliefs, but at helping creatures survive. If that were the case, then why should we trust our idea that we are the product of purely random factors? According to that very idea, the mental processes leading to this conclusion would not be aimed at producing true beliefs.

Charles Darwin seems to have understood this when he wrote, "With me the horrid doubt always arises whether the convictions of man's mind, which has been developed from the mind of the lower animals, are of any value or at all trustworthy. Would anyone trust in the convictions of a monkey's mind, if there are any convictions in such a mind?"[8]

An atheist could reply to this objection by saying that true beliefs are the ones that are most likely to help us survive, and therefore evolution will give rise to creatures whose minds are ordered toward acquiring true beliefs. This reply does not overcome the problem, though, because it's obviously possible that we could survive even if we accrued many false beliefs about subjects that don't relate to our survival (such as the atomic structure of objects around us). But the worry that we can't trust our own minds disappears if God was guiding the development of the human mind so that it was aimed at knowing him, and thus knowing the truth.

9. Doesn't the theory of evolution contradict the creation story in the book of Genesis?

The Bible contains many different styles of writing. History, poetry, prophecy, parables, and other literary genres are found in its pages. This is not surprising, since it's not so much a book as a library—a collection of seventy-three books written at different times by different people.

As such it's important that we distinguish among the types of literature within the Bible and what they are trying to tell us. It would be a mistake, for example, to take the Bible's richness of symbolism and literary figures as if these things were always relating truth and history in the manner that we in our culture are accustomed to.

Still less should we expect it to offer accounts that line up with modern scientific modes of expression. If we're hoping to find, for example, a scientific account of creation, we will not find it the Bible, for the Bible was never intended to be a cosmological textbook. This doesn't mean that the Bible errs when it describes the creation of the world, just that it describes it in a particular way for a particular purpose. According to the *Catechism of the Catholic Church,* the creation passages in Genesis "express in their solemn language the truths of creation—its origin and its end in God, its order and goodness, the vocation of man, and finally the drama of sin and the hope of salvation" (289).

St. Augustine put it this way: "We don't read in the gospel that the Lord said, 'I am sending you the Holy Spirit, that he may teach you about the course of the sun and the moon.' He wished to make people Christians not astronomers."[9]

The Catholic Church is open to the idea of an old universe and to the idea that God used evolution as part of his plan for creating life. According to the *Catechism*:

> The question about the origins of the world and of man has been the object of many scientific studies which have splendidly enriched our knowledge of the age and dimensions of the cosmos, the development of life-forms and the appearance of man. These discoveries invite us to even greater admiration for the greatness of the Creator, prompting us to give him thanks for all his works and for the understanding and wisdom he gives to scholars and researchers (283).

Or, as Joseph Cardinal Ratzinger (later Pope Benedict XVI) beautifully put it, the biblical account of man's creation doesn't

> explain how human persons come to be but rather what they are. It explains their inmost origin and casts light on the project that they are. And, vice versa, the theory of evolution seeks to understand and describe biological developments. But in so doing it can't explain where the "project" of human persons comes from, nor their inner origin, nor their particular nature. To that extent we are faced here with two complementary—rather than mutually exclusive—realities.[10]

The recognition that the creation accounts must be understood with some nuance is not new. Christian writers from the early centuries, 1,500 years or more before Darwin, saw the six biblical "days" of creation as something other than literal twenty-four-hour periods.

For example, in the A.D. 200s, Origen of Alexandria noted that day and night are made on the first day but the sun is not created until the fourth. The ancients knew as well as we do that the presence or absence of the sun is what makes it day or night, and so he took this as an indication that the text was using a literary device and not presenting a literal chronology. "I don't suppose," he wrote, "that anyone doubts that these things figuratively indicate certain mysteries, the history having taken place in appearance, and not literally" (*De Principiis* 4:16).

The ancients recognized, long before modern science, that the biblical story of creation does not require us to think that the world was made in exactly six twenty-four-hour days, or that man was formed from dust. Only modern skeptics try to force this novel and literal interpretation on the Bible.

10. You theists say that since everything needs a cause, there must be a God. But if everything needs a cause, then God does too, right?

Theists don't say that *everything* needs a cause—only things that began to exist. Or, to put it another way, that things that can fail to exist need a cause for their existence.

Things that come into being at a certain point in time must have a cause for their existence. But if something exists outside of time—such as God—then it never had a moment where it came into being and so doesn't need a cause.

Likewise, if something *doesn't have to exist,* then we need an explanation for why it does exist. But if something does have to exist—if it's a *necessary being* like God—then it doesn't need an explanation. Existence is simply part of what it is; and God, by definition, is a necessary being that must exist.

To our observation, the things around us in the universe appear to have had a beginning in time, and so they need a cause—a reason why they began to exist in the first place. All those bits of matter in the universe—the stars, blades of grass, the clock on your desk—don't seem to be necessary. They could, in theory, *not* exist. Therefore, we need an explanation for why they do exist.

God, according to the traditional theistic definition, can be the ultimate explanation for these things because he needs no further explanation. Indeed, the question, "Who created God?" is nonsensical, because it amounts to asking, "Who created an uncreated being?"

11. Could God create a rock so heavy that even he could not lift it? Whether the answer is yes or no, it

proves that the idea of an omnipotent God is self-contradictory.

Believers do hold that God is omnipotent (Latin: *omnis,* "all" plus *potens,* "powerful"). But omnipotence doesn't mean that God can do anything—it means he can do anything that is *possible.*

Not all things are logically possible. For example, no artist, no matter how skilled, could draw a square circle or a four-sided triangle. We can speak of such things, but it doesn't mean they're possible; we're just combining words in a way that—if you stop to analyze them—makes no sense at all. We can't draw such objects or even imagine them. An all-powerful God could not make one. They're logical impossibilities.

The idea of an omnipotent being making a rock too heavy for him to lift is another such example. An omnipotent being has an infinite amount of lifting power, so anything too heavy for such a being to lift would have to have more than infinite weight. But "more than infinite" is one of those combinations of words that contain a logical impossibility. It's a nonsense phrase that can't correspond to anything in reality or in our imagination.

To ask the question "Can God create a rock so heavy that he himself could not lift it?" is in effect to ask, "Is God powerful enough to fail?" This is as logically nonsensical as asking, "Can God purple toaster gremlin cupboard?" When asking questions of the form, "Can God X?" whatever stands in for X must be meaningful.

Just as an all-powerful God can't logically overcome his own power, an all-good God can't do things that violate his own goodness. For example, he can't do evil acts or cause others to. Such acts would be contrary to his nature and therefore logically impossible. But in no way does God's inability to do the impossible make him self-contradictory and thus disprove his existence.

12. How can you believe in an all-powerful and all-loving God in the face of so much evil in the world?

The problem of evil is the greatest emotional obstacle to belief in God. It just doesn't *feel* like God should let people suffer. If we were God, we think, we wouldn't allow it.

The atheist philosopher J.L. Mackie maintained that belief in God was irrational, for if God were all-knowing (omniscient), he would know that there was evil in the world; if he were all-powerful (omnipotent), he could prevent it; and if he were all-good (omnibe-nevolent), then he would wish to prevent it. The fact that there is still evil in the world proves that God doesn't exist, or that if he did, he must be "impotent, ignorant, or wicked."

As keenly felt as the problem of evil may be, how-ever, it doesn't represent a strong intellectual or logical obstacle to God's existence. Mackie was wrong: The existence of God and the existence of evil aren't mutually exclusive. Let's look at the three attributes of God that Mackie named.

Omnipotence: As we noted in the prior answer, omnipotence doesn't mean the ability to do what is logically impossible. It's possible, therefore, for God to create beings with the kind of free will that can choose between good and evil, but having done so he can't also force those creatures to choose freely to do good. If he *forced* their choice, it wouldn't be a *free* choice.

Omniscience: If God has infinite knowledge, then he knows many things we don't. This means that he may, in fact, have good reasons for permitting things—such as evil and suffering—that seem inexplicable to us.

Human beings have a very limited vantage point, and so we often lack knowledge of things of true significance. What appears to us to be a tragedy may have effects that bring about great good, and conversely, what appears to us as a good thing may, in the long run, prove harmful. Consider the analogy of a small child being taken to the doctor for his immunization shots. He knows the needle hurts, and he can't understand why his own parents are allowing the doctor to cause him pain—that the inoculations help prevent the much greater suffering of disease. He's unable to perceive the greater good.

Likewise, we should recognize that a being with more knowledge than us—like God—may have good reasons for things, even pain and suffering, that we are unaware of. And so he allows evil to exist because of his omniscience, not in spite of it.

Omnibenevolence: As we think about the goodness of God, we must be careful not to impose on him our inadequate understandings of what goodness is. In his book *The Problem of Pain*, the English author C.S. Lewis writes:

> By the goodness of God we mean nowadays almost exclusively his lovingness; and in this we may be right. And by love, in this context, most of us mean kindness. . . . What would really satisfy would be a God who said of anything we happened to like doing, "What does it matter so long as they are contended." We want, in fact, not so much a Father in heaven as a grandfather in heaven—a senile benevolence who, as they say, "liked to see young people enjoying themselves" and whose plan for the universe was simply that it might be truly said at the end of each day, "a good time was had by all."[11]

Furthermore, most theists don't believe that God created us merely for happiness in this life, but also— and more importantly—for eternal happiness with him in the next. So, his omnibenevolence should be judged neither by our limited human standards of goodness nor by what happens in this world alone.

Putting these things together, we can recognize that an omnipotent, omniscient, and omnibenevolent creator might have good reasons for tolerating abuses of human free will that lead to evil and suffering. We may not know what all his reasons are, but we sense the value of freedom, including the value of being able to choose good freely rather than by compulsion. We can see how in both his power and knowledge God can bring good out of evil in ways that we, in our limitations, aren't always able to comprehend. But in faith we can say along with St. Paul, "We know that in everything God works for good with those who love him" (Rom. 8:28).

In fact, rather than disproving God's existence, the reality of evil actually points to it, in an indirect way. If evil exists, then it follows that real morality exists. Why? Because evil, by definition, is that which acts against the good. If there were no objective good, then we could say there are things we dislike, or what we call suffering, but there could be no such thing as evil. Therefore, if objective morality exists, then it follows that God exists. Objective moral laws point to a perfect and unchanging moral law-giver.

We will have more to say about this later on, but for now notice that it's only within a moral framework that the sufferings of this life can have any meaning. It may be a mystery why an all-good God allows suffering and evil to take place, but at least on this view there is meaning and purpose, and God can ultimately bring about justice and draw good out of the sufferings of this life.

13. Why would a God of love and mercy condemn people to hell?

Many theists belong to religions that teach the existence of a place or state of punishment in the afterlife, or hell. The existence of hell is not a pleasant thing to believe in. But then neither is evil, and yet we've seen that evil is logically consistent with the idea of God. Hell is, too.

First we need to make sure that we're clear on what we mean by hell. It's not a cave deep in the earth where people go to burn. The Bible does use images such as fire and darkness to communicate what hell is like, but these images point to the suffering condition of those who have finally rejected God, who is the source of all happiness. Pope John Paul II said that those images "show the complete frustration and emptiness of life without God. Rather than a place, hell indicates the state of those who freely and definitively separate themselves from God, the source of all life and joy."[12]

Those who die having freely separated themselves from God by the way they lived will have their choice respected in the afterlife. God doesn't force himself on them. If we believed in the afterlife but wanted to throw out the doctrine of hell, we would also have to throw out one of two other beliefs:

1. Humans have free will.
2. God is love.

God doesn't wish that "any should perish, but that all should reach repentance" (2 Pet. 3:9). But if humans have free will, then there is the possibility of their rejecting God's love. Thus you might say that God did not create hell. Rather, sin created hell. As Lewis wrote, "There are only two kinds of people in the end: those who say to God, 'Thy will be done,' and those to whom God says, in the end, 'Thy will be done.' All that are in hell, choose it."[13]

We might be tempted to think that a loving God could never let people suffer for eternity in hell. But, far from being inconsistent with God's loving nature, hell is a necessary consequence of it. Because God is love, he respects our freedom—*for love is never coercive*. If God forced his love on us, he would not be perfectly loving and thus wouldn't be God.

14. Why is God such a cold-hearted judge in the Old Testament and more of a "pacifist" in the New Testament?

It's true that the Old Testament has accounts of God

commanding armies and judging nations that aren't found in the New Testament. But the portraits of God found in the two testaments are not as different as people often think.

In the New Testament, Jesus uses quite dramatic language. Would a pacifist say, "Don't think that I have come to bring peace on earth; I have not come to bring peace, but a sword" (Matt. 10:34)? Or, regarding one who leads others into temptation, would a pacifist say, "It would be better for him if a millstone were hung round his neck and he were cast into the sea, than that he should cause one of these little ones to sin" (Luke 17:2)?

Conversely, a "cold-hearted judge" would not say, "Though your sins are like scarlet, they shall be as white as snow; though they are red like crimson, they shall become like wool" (Isa. 1:18). Neither would he be described as "Father of the fatherless and protector of widows"(Ps. 68:5).

This is not to say that there aren't disturbing passages within Scripture. Indeed, there are. How are we to understand these? Pope Benedict XVI commented on this matter and laid out the basic principles that we need to apply when reading such passages. He pointed out how biblical revelation is deeply rooted in history. God's plan is accomplished slowly, over time, but people resist his plan.

"God chose a people and patiently worked to guide and educate them," Pope Benedict explained. He noted that biblical revelation "is suited to the cultural and moral level of distant times and thus describes facts and customs, such as cheating and trickery, and acts of violence and massacre, without explicitly denouncing the immorality of such things" (*Verbum Domini* 42).

The ancient world was a violent place, just as our own day is. And yet God called the Israelites to something better. He sent the prophets to vigorously challenge injustice and violence, whether collective or individual. This became God's way of training his people in preparation for the gospel. The ultimate key to understanding the entire Bible is Jesus Christ and the love and self-sacrifice that he preached. That is the end point of God's plan, toward which God was leading his people.

15. The only reason you're a Christian is because you were born in the West. If you were born in another part of the world, you'd believe in a different God—or no God at all.

It's certainly true that most people stick close to the belief system that they were trained in as children, and these systems vary from place to place and even from family to family. It's just a fact of history and human nature. But if this is meant to be an argument against God's existence, it is utterly fallacious.

Attempting to invalidate a belief based on how that belief originated is called the genetic fallacy.

Obviously, people may come to hold all sorts of beliefs for inadequate reasons, and those beliefs could still be true. For example, my son learned from a cartoon that you could fit about a million earths into the sun. If I were to say to my son, "That can't be true; you learned it from a cartoon," that would be committing the genetic fallacy.

Applied to God's existence, this faulty logic cuts both ways. If you were an atheist raised in an unbelieving family or in a secular culture, would being a product of your environment invalidate your atheism? Obviously, in neither case does how we were raised tell us whether our beliefs are *true*, which is the real question. In order to get at the answer to that question, you have to look at evidence.

16. Faith has been defined as "believing without seeing." Doesn't that make faith irrational?

It's true that faith is belief in things unseen. St. Paul wrote, "While we are at home in the body we are away from the Lord, for we walk by faith, not by sight" (2 Cor. 5:6).

But this doesn't mean that theists have no rational basis for their beliefs. In fact, reason alone is enough to show us God exists, without any faith. Even the Bible reminds us that we can discern God's existence from the natural world, without any supernatural assistance: "For from the greatness and beauty of created things comes a corresponding perception of their creator" (Wis. 13:4-5). St. Paul himself wrote that God's nature "has been clearly perceived in the things that have been made" (Rom. 1:19-20).

So when St. Paul writes that "we walk by faith, not by sight," he doesn't mean that we can't have a natural, rational knowledge of God, or that this knowledge can't inform and ground the beliefs that we hold by faith. (The Catholic Church even teaches as dogma that God can be known with certainty of human reason.) What Paul means, rather, is that in this life we are called to walk in confident expectation of what God has promised us is to come, and that we are not to become discouraged by trials.

17. Okay, then, so what evidence is there for God's existence?

There are many good reasons to think that God exists. In their book *Handbook of Catholic Apologetics,* Peter Kreeft and Ronald Tacelli outline twenty arguments for the existence of God. In the limited space available here, allow me to sketch briefly three such arguments. (In the resource section at the end of this booklet, I will point you to places where you can find more arguments that go into much greater depth.)

The Kalām Argument

The core of this argument, named after the Islamic philosophical tradition that refined it, can be phrased as follows:

1. Whatever begins to exist has a cause of its existence.
2. The universe began to exist.
3. Therefore, the universe has a cause of its existence: God.

The first premise seems obviously true by our experience. Things don't simply pop into existence, uncaused, out of nothing.[14] Indeed, if anything did appear simply to pop into existence, we would immediately begin asking why—what was the *cause* of this thing?

What about the second premise? Did the universe, all of time, space, matter and energy, begin to exist? Atheists have typically said that the universe exists without explanation and has been here forever. "The universe," claimed Bertrand Russell, "is just there. And that's all." Recent scientific discoveries, however, suggest otherwise. Today the standard view is that the universe—all space and time—sprang into existence around 13.7 billion years ago, in an event called the "Big Bang."

These discoveries tend to put atheists in an awkward position, a position expressed well by former NASA scientist Robert Jastrow, who writes, "For the scientist who has lived by his faith in the power of reason, the story ends like a bad dream. He has scaled the mountain of ignorance; he is about to conquer the highest peak; as he pulls himself over the final rock, he is greeted by a band of theologians who have been sitting there for centuries."[15] Even if our universe emerged from an even larger "multiverse," which caused the Big Bang, scientists concur that even this larger multiverse must also have a finite past.[16] And so we reach our conclusion: Since nothing can begin to exist without a cause, and since the universe began to exist, it follows that there is a cause of the universe.

What can we know about this cause? Since it created space, time, and matter, it must be greater than all those things. Furthermore, it must be personal, not a mere "force." For only a person with free will could create in time what had not been there before. As philosopher William Lane Craig put it,

> How else could a timeless cause give rise to a temporal effect like the universe? If the cause were an impersonal set of necessary and sufficient conditions, then the cause could never exist without the effect. If the cause were eternally present, then the effect would be eternally present as well. The only way for the cause to be timeless and the effect to begin in time is for the cause to be a personal agent who freely chooses to create an effect in time without any prior determining conditions. Thus, we are

brought, not merely to a transcendent cause of the universe, but to its personal creator.[17]

The Kalām argument demonstrates the existence of an uncaused, spaceless, timeless, immaterial, all-powerful, personal creator of the universe. That sounds a lot like God.

The Contingency Argument

Our next argument goes like this:

1. Whatever exists that does not have to exist requires an explanation for its existence.
2. The physical universe does not have to exist.
3. Therefore, the universe requires an explanation in something that must exist.
4. God is the only being that must exist.
5. Therefore, God is the explanation for the existence of the universe.

The first premise of this argument reflects the human perception that there are reasons for the existence of the things we see around us. This is what drives science, as well as every other branch of study. It's the great question: "Why?" This question applies to anything that doesn't have to exist or that could be different from what it is (what philosophers sometimes refer to as "contingent" things).

For example, when astronomers discovered red-colored stars, they tried to explain their existence. To say that there isn't an explanation—not that we don't know it but that there actually *isn't* one—strikes at the foundation of rational thought. It's to reject the whole premise that underlies the quest for knowledge. The first premise of our argument thus seems secure.

So does the second premise. If we look around the physical universe, we see it filled with stars and galaxies. And we see that the things within it obey certain laws and those physical laws have certain constants, or unchanging values. For example, the constant C in $E=MC^2$ refers to the speed of light, or 186,000 miles per second. This fact about light never changes, and so it is called a constant. There are many other constants, such as the gravitational constant: Gravity is so strong and not stronger or weaker. We experience three dimensions of space and one of time, not more or less.

Why?

At one time the universe didn't contain stars and galaxies. Why do those objects exist now when they clearly don't have to? All of these matters are subjects of scientific inquiry, and they reveal that the physical universe as a whole is contingent. That is, the universe is one way but could be another, or it could simply not be at all. It therefore needs a reason for its own existence—an explanation.

But let's inquire a bit further and ask about what *could* explain the way the physical universe is. Whatever it is, it must be greater than the physical universe; it must be something beyond space and time, beyond matter and energy, but with the power to create each of these and to establish the laws that they obey. It would be something that explains its own existence and could not fail to exist.

Once again, that sounds a lot like God: what philosophers call a "necessary" being: God could not be different from what he is, which is what premise 3 states.

This is something our intuition also tells us. There must be an ultimate explanation, one that doesn't depend on anything else, and thus one that explains everything else. There must be something fundamental, something that grounds all the contingent things we see around us. And thus there must be a God.

The Moral Argument

The third argument says:

1. If God doesn't exist, then objective moral values don't exist.
2. Objective moral values do exist.
3. Therefore, God exists.

The first premise is something that Christians

and atheists may agree about. As we saw earlier, many Christians have argued that if God didn't exist, there could not be a rational basis for objective morality. Many atheists have said, yes, since there's no God, morality is a human construct. Good and evil aren't real—they're just words we use, concepts we've invented.

For example, the atheist philosopher Michael Ruse wrote that morality "is a biological adaptation no less than are hands and feet and teeth." It is "just an aid to survival and reproduction," and consequently, "any deeper meaning is illusory."[18]

But the second premise is that objective moral values and duties *do* exist. And if we're honest, mustn't we acknowledge this? When we hear stories of horrible crimes, for example, murders committed by a serial killer, we don't think, "A biological adaptation is causing me to apply feelings of disapproval toward these acts."

No, we think that these crimes are *evil,* because murder is *wrong*—not "wrong for me but perhaps right for you," but simply wrong in itself.

The intuition that such moral values are real is so deeply embedded in the human heart that even those who deny objective morality invariably can be found making moral judgments and expressing moral outrage. Ruse, who thinks morality is a "biological adaptation," wrote elsewhere, "The man who says that it is morally acceptable to rape little children is just as mistaken as the man who says, 2+2=5."[19]

So, the question is not whether objective morality exists, but what the basis for it might be. Here are four possibilities:

Nature

- Moral laws could be part of the natural world, like the laws of physics. In that case they would be something that the natural sciences could detect. Yet they don't seem to be. You can't measure good and evil in a scientific experiment. Furthermore, we don't say that animals are acting immorally when they kill or steal from each other. Why doesn't our morality apply to them, too, just as the laws of physics do? Morality must therefore transcend the natural world and the realm of science.

Individual Choice

- Perhaps we make our own morality, according to our choices. All of us, after all, have our own consciences and personal moral beliefs. This, however, wouldn't explain how things could be right or wrong even apart from (or in contradiction to) my choices. It also wouldn't result in a set of moral values that are binding on other people. What I think is right and wrong wouldn't apply to you. (Or, if I happened to change my mind, to me!)

Society

- Perhaps moral values are established by what society

decides and expresses through customs and laws. In other words, what is legal and acceptable is therefore moral. But this is really just a collective version of the individual choice idea, and so it too fails to establish a truly objective and binding set of moral values. What if I disagree with society? What right do others have to tell me what I should and shouldn't do? What if a society approves of something—like slavery or the Holocaust—that we consider clearly immoral?

God

- Finally, objective morality might be grounded in God—flowing from his own nature and goodness, as well as his authority to prescribe certain kinds of behavior. This seems to make sense; for only if morality originates in something *above* me would it have *authority* over me—the right to tell me what to do and what not to do. As Francis J. Beckwith and Greg Koukl observe: "A command only makes sense when there are two minds involved, one giving the command and one receiving it."[20] If an objective moral law is indeed a command that we receive, then there must be an objective, personal moral commander beyond nature, the individual, or society.

Thus, it seems that apart from God there is no objective foundation for morality. This doesn't mean that *belief* in God is necessary to act morally; just that

God—a perfectly good, transcendent lawgiver—is the only thing we can logically point to as a basis for saying that some things *are* just right or wrong.

18. Maybe God does exist, but that doesn't mean that Christianity is true.

It's true that arguments for God's existence don't prove that Christianity is true. (Instead they point to a kind of "mere theism.") Along with believing that God exists, Christianity teaches that Jesus of Nazareth was the Messiah expected by the Jewish people and that he was fully divine and fully human. It bases this belief on Jesus' own words, as reported in the Gospels.

Throughout history some have tried to portray Jesus as merely a good and wise man; a teacher, a sage. Others have viewed him as a kind of prophet or mystic. But Jesus claimed more than this: He claimed to be God himself.

For example, in John 8:58 Jesus applies the divine name (which Jews dared not even pronounce) to himself, saying that before the prophet Abraham—who lived thousands of years before—existed, "I AM." This statement throws the Jewish high priests into a frenzy and motivates them to kill Jesus for blasphemy. In John 20:28 Thomas speaks to the resurrected Jesus and says, "My Lord and my God." Jesus, who like all good Jews knew there could be only one God, does not correct

Thomas for uttering what would have been blasphemy if it were not true.

The divinity of Christ is indeed a striking claim, and it's either true or false. If it's true, then he is God (however great a mystery this is), and the core of the Christian faith is true. If what he said about himself is false, on the other hand, then it's hardly possible to call this bold liar a good or wise man.

So that leaves us with three alternatives:

1. He was a liar, a religious phony who duped people into believing in him.
2. He was a lunatic, sincere perhaps but seriously deluded.
3. He was a mere legend who didn't exist at all.

The Liar Hypothesis

If Jesus was a liar, then it follows that he was a bad man, for no good man would deceive others about his identity, encouraging them to worship him (Matt. 28:17) and causing them leave everything to follow him (Luke 5:11).

A problem with this option, however, is that no one who reads the life of Christ can reasonably find him to be a bad man. He feeds the hungry (Matt. 14:13-21), comforts the sorrowful (Luke 23:27-29), shows compassion to those living immoral lives (John 8:2-11), indeed he commands his followers to clothe the naked, care for the sick, visit those in prison (Matt. 25:31-46). By all accounts, Jesus of Nazareth was a morally enlightened individual.

The Lunatic Hypothesis

What about the second option? Perhaps Jesus sincerely but erroneously believed himself to be God.

It's certainly possible—insane asylums are full of such people.

But when we read about Jesus, does he come across as a crazy person? Not to most readers. He doesn't do anything insane. His teachings are wise, balanced, and smart—not the irrational rantings of a lunatic. Those who knew him, and billions who came to follow him, quite evidently found him to be sage and convincing, not crazy.

Read the words of the Sermon on the Mount in Matthew 5:1-10 and ask yourself, could these really be the words of an insane man?

The Legend Hypothesis

Still others have claimed that Jesus never even existed, or that if he did exist, so much legend has grown around him that we can't trust the New Testament documents that describe his life and teachings. We have no way of sorting out what he really said and did from what was later falsely attributed to him.

But this argument fails to account for just how reliable the accounts of Jesus are. The majority of the books of the New Testament were written within the first generation after his crucifixion, while most of the eyewitnesses of Jesus' ministry were still alive. This gives us better sources for Jesus than we have for most of the major figures of ancient history. Our earliest biographies of Alexander the Great, for example, were written 400 years after his death—yet historians don't doubt that Alexander the Great existed or that we have a basically accurate knowledge of his life.

New Testament documents are better attested to than any other works of antiquity. We have 500 manuscripts that are dated earlier than A.D. 500, whereas the next best attested-to ancient text is Homer's epic poem the *Iliad*, of which we know of only fifty copies that date within 500 years of its origin. This quantity of New Testament manuscripts enables us to check them against each other and ensure that they have been reliably transmitted to us, with very few variant readings. This means that they reliably communicate their original message and are not a conglomeration of legends that built up slowly over time.

You can read about Jesus of Nazareth, Pontius Pilate, and even John the Baptist in nonbiblical sources of the period, such as the writings of the Jewish historian Flavius Josephus (A.D. 37–c. 100). Other early authors who make reference to Jesus and the early Christian community include the Roman official Pliny the Younger (61–c. 112) and the Roman historians Tacitus (56 –117) and Suetonius (c. 69–c. 122).

To say that the apostles made up the story of Jesus' life, death, and resurrection, you must also be willing to say that they endured horribly painful deaths, including being flayed alive, crucified, stoned, and beheaded, for what they knew to be a lie. Not to mention, such elaborate conspiracies are hard to keep covered up. The fourth-century historian Eusebius made this very observation, noting that if the story of Jesus was made up, "what a wonder it is that such a number were able to keep to their agreement about their fabrication, even in the face of death, and that no coward among them ever retired from the association and made a premature repudiation of the things agreed upon; nor did they ever announce anything in contradiction to the others, bringing to light what had been put together among themselves."

These, and many other reasons, make it clear why the idea that Jesus never existed is more the stuff of Internet forums and amateur bloggers than serious historians—almost none of whom give any serious credence to it.

So if Jesus could not have been a liar, a lunatic, or a legendary figure, then logically we must be prepared to accept him as what he claimed to be—the God of the universe. Calling him a good and wise moral leader simply is not an option.

"You must make your choice," C.S. Lewis wrote. "Either this man was, and is, the Son of God: or else a madman or something worse. You can shut Him up for a fool, you can spit at Him and kill Him as a demon; or you can fall at His feet and call Him Lord and God. But let us not come with any patronizing nonsense about His being a great human teacher. He has not left that open to us. He didn't intend to."[21]

19. Many different religions tell myth stories, some of them about dying and rising gods. Isn't Jesus just a spinoff of these pagan myths?

Before we look at some of these alleged parallels between Christianity and paganism (and why they're false), it's important to note that similarity does not imply dependence. That is, even if Christianity did have beliefs and practices similar to those of earlier religions, it doesn't follow that there must be a causal connection between them.

Similarities among religions shouldn't surprise us. Most religions, after all, try to answer the same fundamental questions in life: "Where did we come from?" "Is there an afterlife?" How should we live?" Most religions have rituals, sacred stories, and moral codes. It would be surprising if there *weren't* some similarities among them. In fact, you might say that the similarities are a sign that God does exist—you might expect different religions in different eras and cultures to reach many similar conclusions about what he's like and how to relate to him.

Claims that Christian beliefs about Jesus are adapted from pagan cults may be popular today, but they're nothing new. A school of nineteenth-century German theologians sought to interpret Jesus against a pagan background rather than a Jewish one, perhaps due to the anti-Semitic desire for an Aryan Jesus. The movement continued into the early twentieth century, with writers who sought to deny the historicity of Christ by drawing upon the work of liberal German theologians. But mainstream scholarship did not take these critics seriously, and their works fell into relative obscurity.

It was not until the 1970s, when a British professor named Wells translated these works into English, that "mythicism" rose to prominence. However, it is still relatively a fringe movement, and even Wells has abandoned it, admitting there is a historical basis for the stories about Jesus.[22] Even agnostics such as Bart Ehrman, who has become popular for his arguments against the reliability of the New Testament, admit that Jesus was a real historical figure, writing, "The view that Jesus existed is held by virtually every expert on the planet."[23]

But the popular impact of mythicism continues and so deserves to be addressed. Among the many ancient pagan deities of which Christ is said to be a copy, the Egyptian god Horus seems to get the most attention. Although much could be said about each of the alleged parallels between Jesus and Horus, due to our limited space we will examine three: 1. Horus's virgin birth, 2. his crucifixion, and 3. his resurrection.

1. "Horus was born to a virgin mother."

Several different (and contradictory) stories about Horus have developed gradually over the last 3,000 years, but the most common story of his conception espoused by mythicists today involves his father, Osiris, and mother, Isis. It goes like this: When Osiris was murdered and his body cut up into fourteen pieces, his wife Isis journeyed throughout Egypt collecting them. She was able to find all pieces except his genitals (not making this up), which had been eaten by catfish at the bottom of the Nile. Isis then makes a prosthetic phallus, gets impregnated by it, and along comes Horus.[24]

A virgin birth? Not exactly.

2. Horus was crucified.

How did Horus die? Well, again, that depends on which account you go by. Horus either a) did not die, b) died as a child after having being poisoned by a scorpion, or c) his death is conflated with Osiris's (recounted above). Yet the popular mythicist film *Zeit-geist* claims he was "crucified."

Now, crucifixion was a Roman invention; there was no Egyptian equivalent. So what is the justification for this belief? *There are images of Horus standing with outstretched arms.* That's it. As the film's study guide explains, "The issue at hand is not a man being thrown to the ground and nailed to a cross, as Jesus is depicted to have been, but the portrayal of gods and goddesses in cruciform, where by the divine figure appears with arms outstretched in a symbolic context."[25]

By this line of reasoning we should also conclude that Barney the dinosaur was also crucified, since there are many images of him standing with outstretched arms!

3. Horus rose from the dead.
Though there are many uninformed claims flying around that Jesus' resurrection is borrowed from Horus, the fact is that the dying and revivification of Horus is vastly dissimilar to the death and resurrection of Christ. And the general view that ancient pagan religions were filled with dying and rising gods that the New Testament authors borrowed in order to concoct the story of Christ does not pass scholarly muster. As the *Encyclopedia of Religion* puts it, "The category of dying and rising gods, once a major topic of scholarly investigation, must be understood to have

been largely a misnomer based on imaginative recon-structions. . . . There is no unambiguous instance in the history of religions of a dying and rising deity."[26]

Those who claim that Jesus is just a spinoff of a pagan god should do three important things: 1. Ask, "Where am I getting my information?" If it's from a website or movie, where did it get *its* information? 2. Take the parallels one at a time. It's easy to rattle off a list of alleged parallels, making it appear that the evidence is overwhelming. But if you take the time to examine each supposed parallel, you'll find, as we found above, that they are not very similar at all. 3. Study the alleged parallels from authoritative sourc-es for yourself. Don't take unscholarly claims at face value.

20. How can I decide about God's existence if I'm not sure?

Sometimes, even after much reflection and study, peo-ple still feel that they can't decide between atheism and belief in God. The evidence seems so evenly weighted.

What then?

If it seems impossible to decide between these op-tions based on the evidence, then perhaps you could consider the advantages of choosing one course over the other. That is, what could the results be of your choice? There are four possible scenarios:

1. You choose to live as if God exists, and you're correct: He does exist.
2. You choose to live as if God doesn't exist, and you're incorrect: He does exist.
3. You choose to live as if God exists, and you're incorrect: He doesn't exist.
4. You choose to live as if God doesn't exist, and you're correct: He doesn't exist.

In scenario 1 you stand to receive the infinite good of everlasting life!

If 2 is the case, then you risk missing out on this infinite good.

In the third scenario, what awaits you after this life is not heaven but non-existence, but during life you would enjoy the consolation (and, studies suggest, more health and happiness) that comes from believing God exists. What would it matter that you were wrong? You wouldn't exist anymore.

In the last case you'd be right about God's non-existence, but what difference would that make after you were dead? Meanwhile you would miss out on the all the benefits of believing in God and practicing religion: including a sense of meaning and purpose in life that would be absent if you believed we're just walking bags of chemicals.

Of these four options, believing in God offers either small or great rewards with little risk, whereas not believing poses potentially great risk with little reward. That being the case, when the evidence leaves you torn between belief and unbelief, the rational choice is to believe. Even basic self-interest, which is certainly part of human nature whether you believe God built it into us or not, clearly points toward believing in God.

Bear in mind that this is not an argument for God's existence but rather an argument for *believing* in God's existence. It's also not an argument for every possible situation. It's designed for those who feel torn between atheism and belief in the kind of God that Christianity proposes but who aren't at a point where they feel that they can settle the question by objective evidence. If you're in that situation, then this argument can help you.

If you think about it, there are many times in life when we must make decisions about what we will believe without having conclusive proof. If we waited, for example, to have conclusive proof that a prospective spouse will always be faithful and never betray us, we'd never get married. In fact, trying to get that kind of proof would likely crush the relationship before we could even get engaged! No, at some point we must make a leap of faith (and trust) and make the commitment, even without total proof.

Remember that no one is ever totally free of doubts. The question isn't whether you have them, but whether you'll let them challenge your commitment. As Lewis wrote, faith is not the absence of doubt, but "the art of holding on to things your reason has once accepted, in spite of your changing moods."[27]

If we were to change our beliefs whenever we have feelings of doubt, we wouldn't get very far in the pursuit of truth. When we recognize that doubts and fears can be random and temporary emotions, it helps us to set them aside and not be thrown into a tailspin. They will pass, and our fundamental commitment to our beliefs will remain. We can keep acting on the premise that God exists, that he loves us, and that we want to please him.

It's also important to remember that, if all that's true, we're not in this alone. We can entrust ourselves to God, to guide and illuminate us.

Here are four ways to grow in your faith, especially when having doubts:

Study: Learn more about Christianity and what the great saints and Christian writers had to say about faith and doubt. You may be edified—and surprised— at what you find.

Read the Bible: Begin with one of the Gospels in the New Testament, such as Luke or John, and gradually make your way through the New Testament, which is the part of the Bible most directly applicable to us today.

The Bible is not simply words about God, but the word *of* God, and the more you study it, the more you will learn about God and the way he interacts with us.

Pray: Set aside a portion of time daily for personal prayer. You might spend this time conversing with God, telling him your fears and hopes in your own words and then spending some time in silence. You also might consider learning some structured prayers, such as the Lord's Prayer, which Jesus himself taught us to say. Or, if you're skeptical, you might pray, as I once prayed, "Lord, if you're real, would you reveal yourself to me in a way that I would understand?"

Get involved: God made us social creatures. We are meant to be with other people, to help them, and to receive help from them. That applies to our faith life as much as anything else. That is why Jesus founded a Church.

So get involved in your local church. Meet other Christians, and become part of the local Christian community. Take an inquirer's class. Go to Bible studies. Join a teen or young adult group. Go to church on Sundays. If you're Catholic, receive the sacraments, such as confession and the Holy Eucharist.

Conclusion: What Now?

Over a decade has passed since I ceased being an agnostic and embraced Christianity. That decision was the most life-changing decision I ever made. I came to know not only that God exists, but that he loves me and sent his son to die for me so that I might come into a relationship with him and so find eternal life. If you had told the younger me that I would someday write those words, I would have told you that you were nuts! Looking back, I see that it wasn't that I found Christianity too *hard* to believe, but too *good*! Everything else in life I had pursued in order to be happy had let me down, so what were the chances that the Christian message could be that good and also be true? Yet I've come to believe that it is. I can honestly say that I find in Christianity the one coherent philosophy and, ultimately, the only satisfying answer.

Resources

Regardless of where you are in your journey, the following resources can help you tremendously:

Websites
- www.catholic.com is the number-one site on the Web when it comes to Catholic apologetics. Catholic.com has the largest online Catholic forum in the world, and it's free to join!
- Also, be sure to check out the Catholic Answers Live podcast. It's a daily, two-hour radio program dedicated to Catholic apologetics and evangelization.

Visit www.Catholic.com/radio to listen or download. (It's also available for free in the iTunes store.)

- www.strangenotions.com is a website for Catholics and atheists interested in discussing the big questions of life.
- www.catholicscomehome.org is a website for those who were once Catholic and want to come back to the Church.
- www.peterkreeft.com is the official website of Peter Kreeft, a professor of philosophy at Boston College. His website has some amazing articles and lectures dealing with the existence of God.
- Many great debates on the existence of God can be found on YouTube. For one great example, search for "William Lane Craig vs. Christopher Hitchens."

Books

- For a comprehensive overview of what the Catholic Church teaches, see the *Catechism of the Catholic Church*, also available online at www.vatican.va. You might also want to check out the shorter *Compendium of the Catechism of the Catholic Church* or *You-Cat*, a catechism specially written for young people, with an introduction by Pope Benedict XVI.
- Catechisms explain what the Church believes, but they don't typically go deep with arguments or evidence. They largely stick to explanations. If you want arguments for the Faith, then you want a work

of apologetics. For a particularly good one (that includes twenty arguments for the existence of God), be sure to pick up a copy of *Handbook of Catholic Apologetics* by Peter J. Kreeft and Ronald K. Tacelli.

- If you're looking for a concise training manual on how to argue for God's existence, I would highly recommend *On Guard* by William Lane Craig.
- For a comprehensive book that answers common objections to the Catholic Faith, I can think of no better book than *The Essential Catholic Survival Guide*, published by Catholic Answers.
- If you would like to delve further into the relationship between faith and reason, then be sure to check out Pope John Paul II's encyclical *Fides et Ratio* ("Faith and Reason"), which you can find for free on the Vatican's website (www.vatican.va).

Endnotes

1   Bertrand Russell, *Why I Am Not a Christian* (New York: Simon and Schuster, 1957), 107.

2   Jean-Paul Sartre, "Existentialism Is a Humanism" (1946).

3   Richard Dawkins, *River out of Eden: A Darwinian View of Life* (New York: Basic Books, 1996), 133.

4   "Is Science a Religion?", http://www.thehumanist.org/humanist/ articles/dawkins.html.

5   "Intelligent Design: Humans, Cockroaches, and the Laws of Physics," http://www.talkorigins.org/faqs/cosmo.html.

6   Peter J. Kreeft and Ronald K. Tacelli, *Handbook of Catholic Apologetics: Reasoned Answers to Questions of Faith* (San Francisco: Ignatius Press, 2009).

7   Jay J. Gould, "Impeaching a Self-Appointed Judge," *Scientific American* 267, no. 1 (1992): 118-121.

8   Charles Darwin, *The Life and Letters of Charles Darwin Including an Autobiographical Chapter*, ed. Francis Darwin (New York: D. Appleton and Company, 1898).

9   *Answer to Felix, a Manichean* 1:10.

10   Joseph Razinger, *In the Beginning* (Grand Rapids: Wm. B. Eerdmans Publishing, 1995).

11   C.S. Lewis, *The Problem of Pain* (New York: The Macmillian Company), 1947.

12   General Audience, July 28, 1999.

13   C.S. Lewis, *The Great Divorce* (San Francisco: HarperSanFrancisco, 2001).

14   Some (such as Lawrence Krauss, Quentin Smith, and others)

have argued that physics gives examples of particles coming into existence out of nothing and that we therefore have grounds for thinking that the universe came into existence out of nothing. This is misleading and inaccurate. The "nothing" they are referring to is not nothing, but rather, the quantum vacuum which "is not truly empty but instead contains fleeting electromagnetic waves and particles that pop into and out of existence" (http://www.aip.org/pnu/1996/split/pnu300-3.htm).

15 Robert Jastrow, *God and the Astronomers* (Toronto: George J. McCleod, 1992).

16 Arvind Borde, Alan H. Guth, and Alexander Vilenkin, "Inflationary Spacetimes Are Not Past-Complete" (Cornell University Library, General Relativity and Quantum Cosmology, 2003), http://arxiv.org/abs/grqc/0110012.

17 William L. Craig, "What Is the Relation between Science and Religion?" Reasonable Faith, http://www.reasonablefaith.org/.

18 Michael Ruse, "Evolutionary Theory and Christian Ethics: Are They in Harmony?" *Zygon* 29, no. 1 (1994), http://philpapers.org/rec/RUSETA.

19 Michael Ruse, *Darwinism Defended* (London: Addison-Wesley, 1982), 275.

20 Francis J. Beckwith and Gregory Koukl, *Moral Relativism: Feet Firmly Planted in Mid-Air* (Grand Rapids: Baker, 1998), 166.

21 C.S. Lewis, *Mere Christianity* (San Fransico: HarperSanFrancisco, 2001), 52.

22 George Albert Wells, *Can We Trust the New Testament?* (Chicago: Open Court, 2004), 43.

23 Bart Ehrman, *Did Jesus Exist?* (New York: HarperOne, 2012), 4.

24 For an authoritative and thorough reference to ancient Egyptian myth, see *The Oxford History of Ancient Egypt*.

25 *Zeitgeist: The Movie Companion Source Guide*, http://www. zeitgeistmovie.com/Zeitgeist,%20The%20Movie-%20 Companion%20Guide%20PDF.pdf.

26 Cited in Jonathan Z. Smith, "Dying and Rising Gods," *Encyclopedia of Religion*, 2nd ed., ed. Lindsay Jones, (Detroit: Macmillan, 2005), 4:2535.

27 Lewis, *Mere Christianity*, 140.

Matt Fradd is a Catholic apologist and chastity speaker. He works with the Internet-accountability company Covenant Eyes, to help protect families from online pornography and assist individuals in overcoming porn addiction.

Become part of the team.
Help support Catholic Answers.

Catholic Answers is an apostolate dedicated to serving Christ by bringing the fullness of Catholic truth to the world. We help good Catholics become better Catholics, bring former Catholics "home," and lead non-Catholics into the fullness of the Faith.

Catholic Answers neither asks for nor receives financial support from any diocese. The majority of its annual income is in the form of donations from individual supporters like you.

To make a donation by phone using your credit card, please speak with one of our customer service representatives at 888-291-8000.

To make a donation by check, please send a check payable to "Catholic Answers" to:

> Catholic Answers
> 2020 Gillespie Way
> El Cajon, CA 92020

To make a donation online, visit **catholic.com**.

TO EXPLAIN & DEFEND THE FAITH

catholic.com